Outdoor

for
Fin and Fowl

Lowfat Recipes

By
Sherri Eldridge

Illustrations by
Rob Groves

Outdoor Grill for Fin and Fowl

Published by:
Harvest Hill Press
P.O. Box 55, Salisbury Cove, Maine 04672
207-288-8900

www.harvesthillpress.com

ISBN: 978-1-886862-19-7

Fourth printing: August 2007

Printed in Canada
on environmentally-friendly
Chlorine-Free and Acid-Free paper

The recipes in this book were created with the goal of reducing fat, calories, cholesterol and sodium. They also present a variety of fresh healthy foods, to be prepared with love and eaten with pleasure.

Credits:

Cover: Cotton print border gratefully used as a courtesy of:
P & B Textiles

Cover Design, Layout and Typesetting: Sherri Eldridge

Front Cover Watercolor and Text Line Art: Robert Groves

Text Typesetting and Proofreading: Bill Eldridge

PREFACE

Everything tastes better when cooked on the grill. It might be something from our heritage that evokes delight in the taste that comes only from grilling. Humans have been grilling their food since the dawn of man, when we conquered fire and sealed our love for fireside cooking.

While the natives of Texas, the Carolinas, Alabama and Kansas have long extolled the virtues of barbecue, the thrill of fresh barbecue has only recently reached the other parts of the country.

What makes grilling so tasty and how is it distinguished from other cooking methods? Basically, grilled food is placed within several inches of the direct heat of a fire and is cooked by conduction. The process sears the outside of the food while concentrating the juices in the center. During the searing process, the food reacts to the heat. The outer layer of carbohydrates is broken down and browns, concentrating the flavor of the food on the exterior. Cooking by grilling even has a scientific name and is called the Maillard reaction, after the French scientist who discovered it.

The intense heat of grilling can only be sustained for so long before the food turns to ashes. The best grilled foods are tender and cook relatively quickly, searing in their juices and flavor.

CONTENTS

Outdoor Cornbread Bake

1 cup unbleached flour
1½ tablespoons baking
 powder
1 tablespoon brown sugar
1 cup cornmeal
1¾ cups skim milk
1 egg, beaten
1 egg white, beaten
1½ tablespoons canola oil

Serving: 1 Wedge	Calories: 179
Protein: 6 gm	Fat: 3.5 gm
Carbs: 30 gm	Cholesterol: 27 mg
Sodium: 269 mg	Calcium: 164 mg

SERVES 8

Prepare grill: Build fire and let it burn to hot coals. Select a cast-iron skillet or grilling pan. Place two bricks on grill, as far apart as possible, but close enough to balance sides of skillet or pan. Cover grill and heat bricks.

Spray skillet or pan with nonstick oil. In a medium bowl, sift together flour, baking powder and brown sugar. Stir in cornmeal, milk, eggs and oil. Pour into prepared skillet or pan.

Place pan on bricks, cover grill. Frequently check cornbread after first 20 minutes by inserting a toothpick in center of cornbread; it is done when toothpick comes out clean or top is golden brown. Cut into 8 wedges, like a pie, serve hot.

Grilled Eggplant
with Garlic Mayonnaise

SERVES 4

5 cloves garlic, minced
2 tablespoons peanut or
    sesame oil
¼ cup rice wine vinegar
½ cup nonfat mayonnaise
2 teaspoons light miso or
    soy sauce
½ teaspoon sugar
1 teaspoon ground ginger
12 baby eggplants
pinch of salt
pinch of pepper
½ head green cabbage,
    finely sliced

Serving: 1/4 Recipe   Calories: 150
Protein: 3 gm   Fat: 7.5 gm
Carbs: 19 gm   Cholesterol: 0 mg
Sodium: 200 mg   Calcium: 70 mg

In a small saucepan, sauté garlic in a tablespoon of oil. Remove from heat and whisk in vinegar, mayonnaise, miso or soy sauce, sugar and ginger.

Cut eggplants in half lengthwise, brush them with the remaining tablespoon of oil, and sprinkle with salt and pepper. Lightly steam cabbage over boiling water, until wilted, drain.

Remove grill from flames and spray with nonstick oil. Grill eggplants skin side up until golden brown, about 3-4 minutes. Turn and grill an additional 2 minutes. Transfer grilled eggplants to plates covered with a bed of wilted cabbage. Spoon Garlic Mayonnaise over eggplants and cabbage, serve hot.

Grilled Corn

Remember that for every hour that passes from the time the corn is picked until you eat it, there is less sugar and more starch.

freshly harvested corn
   left in the husk

butter

salt (optional)

Serving: 2 Ears
Protein: 3 gm
Carbs: 19 gm
Sodium: 76 mg

Calories: 88
Fat: 1.5 gm
Cholesterol: 1 mg
Calcium: 2 mg

2 EARS PER PERSON

Pull down corn husks just far enough to remove silk. After removing silk, run water over corn ear, drain, then close up husk and twist shut.

Roast ears over hot coals, or in 400° oven, 20 minutes or until tender, occasionally turning ears over.

In a tall pot, heat 10 inches of water, butter and salt. Pull back husk and dangle ear from husk. Dip ear in hot buttered water and a thin film of butter will coat the corn. Allow excess water and butter to drip back into the pot.

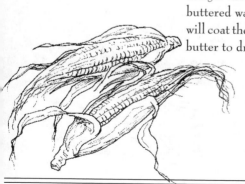

Roasted Peppers and Onions

assortment of sweet, hot
    savory peppers and chilies
assortment of sweet and
    pungent unpeeled onions
olive oil
pinch of pepper
fresh herbs such as basil,
    thyme, parsley, chives,
    and minced garlic

Serving: 1/5 Recipe   Calories: 84
Protein: 2 gm   Fat: 3 gm
Carbs: 14 gm   Cholesterol: 0 mg
Sodium: 5 mg   Calcium: 28 mg

1 LB. PEPPERS AND ONIONS
SERVES 5

Prepare grill and allow to burn to hot coals, or preheat broiler. Remove grill from flames and spray with nonstick oil. Lightly coat peppers, chilies and unpeeled onions in olive oil. Place on grill or under broiler, turning frequently and mashing with spatula. They will char and blacken, but let them cook through, then remove from heat.

Use a damp cloth towel to rub charred skin off peppers, then seed and slice. Peel and slice onions. Sprinkle with olive oil, pepper, and your choice of fresh herbs. Serve at once, or place in covered container and chill.

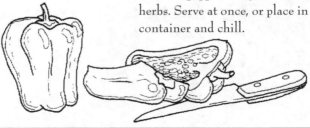

Honey-Glazed Sweet Potatoes

4 medium sweet potatoes
1 tablespoon canola oil

Sauce:
4 tablespoons honey
juice of half an orange
1 tablespoon melted butter
pinch of allspice
¼ teaspoon salt

SERVES 4

Serving: 1 Potato	Calories: 245
Protein: 2 gm	Fat: 6.5 gm
Carbs: 47 gm	Cholesterol: 8 mg
Sodium: 189 mg	Calcium: 36 mg

Peel sweet potatoes and slice lengthwise into ½-inch-thick slices. Boil in a large pot of water just until cooked, but still firm, about 10 minutes. Drain and cool to room temperature. Brush with oil.

While the sweet potato slices are cooling, mix sauce ingredients in a small bowl.

Remove grill from flames and spray with nonstick oil. Over a moderately hot fire, place sweet potato slices on grill and cook until slightly brown on each side, about 3 minutes. Brush with honey sauce and cook very briefly, about 30 seconds on each side, just until glazed.

Grills and Equipment

There are all sizes and shapes of grills that you can buy and use. The most basic is the pit barbecue. This is nothing more than a pit in the ground with a grill or bars laid over it, upon which food can be cooked. More elaborate versions have a spit and motor to turn the food as it cooks. The most simple grill is the brazier which includes the hibachi style. The more elaborate of these have covers or hoods to dampen and control the fire and can include a motorized spit. Some even have electrical or gas heating elements. This technique has even been extended into the house where a gas or electric grill is part of the stove. Finally, there is the yiro from the middle east, a vertical, motorized spit with the embers packed into half a cylinder around the spit.

No special equipment is needed to grill. If you do decide to buy equipment, purchase a long-handled fork; a heavy-duty, long-handled spring-loaded tong; a large, quality paint brush; and long-handled spatula. A fish basket for grilling fish, and flat double-edged skewers for kabobs are also useful. Have a handy work area with a table near the grill for platters, sauces, equipment, etc. And for safety's sake, always have a ready water source like a

BBQ Salsa Sauce

2 tablespoons canola oil
2 cloves garlic, minced
1 medium onion, chopped
2 large tomatoes, peeled
   and chopped
1-2 small fresh hot chiles,
   seeded and finely chopped
3 tablespoons wine vinegar
¼ cup crushed tomatoes
1 teaspoon brown sugar
½ teaspoon salt
½ teaspoon black pepper
3 tablespoons fresh chopped
   cilantro (coriander)

MAKES 1 CUP

Heat oil in saucepan, sauté garlic and onion until tender. Add remaining salsa ingredients, except cilantro. Simmer 20 minutes, stirring occasionally. Adjust seasonings. Stir in cilantro and cook 1 minute more. Serve hot or cold.

Serving: 2 Tablespoons
Protein: 1 gm
Carbs: 4 gm
Sodium: 77 mg

Calories: 50
Fat: 3.5 gm
Cholesterol: 0 mg
Calcium: 9 mg

Sweet & Hot Orange Paste

2 large yellow onions,
   thickly sliced
3 tablespoons fresh seeded
   and chopped hot chiles
1 clove garlic, minced
4 tablespoons peanut oil
¼ cup chopped dried
   apricots
½ cup white wine
¼ cup white vinegar
¼ cup orange marmalade
¼ teaspoon salt
¼ teaspoon pepper
2 medium-sized oranges

MAKES 2 CUPS

Sauté onions, chilies and garlic in oil over medium-high heat until onion is golden. Add apricots, wine and vinegar to saucepan, cook 20 minutes more.

Stir in marmalade, salt and pepper. Halve and seed the oranges. Scoop out pulp and add to saucepan. Cook down until thickened into paste. Use to coat and baste fish or fowl 2 minutes before removing from grill.

Serving: 2 Tablespoons	Calories: 66
Protein: 0 gm	Fat: 3.5 gm
Carbs: 8 gm	Cholesterol: 0 mg
Sodium: 38 mg	Calcium: 12 mg

Kickin' Chicken BBQ

1 medium onion
2 teaspoons canola oil
1½ cups catsup
1 cup red wine
½ cup cider vinegar
¼ cup packed brown sugar
2 teaspoons lemon juice
2 tablespoons
   Worcestershire sauce
½ teaspoon liquid smoke
pinch or more of cayenne
1 teaspoon ground ginger
1 tablespoon garlic powder
1 bay leaf
½ teaspoon salt
½ teaspoon black pepper
2 tablespoons flour
lean skinned chicken

MAKES 3 CUPS SAUCE

Dice onion into small pieces. In a large saucepan, sauté onion in oil. Whisk in remaining ingredients, and simmer 30 minutes or until thickened. Remove bay leaf.

Remove grill from flames and spray with nonstick oil. Grill chicken on barbecue. When almost cooked through, baste with a thick coat of sauce, turn and baste second side. Continue basting and turning to cover in three coats of barbecue sauce, being careful that sauce does not burn. Serve with extra sauce on the side.

Serving: 2 Tablespoons   Calories: 39
Protein: 1 gm   Fat: 0.5 gm
Carbs: 9 gm   Cholesterol: 0 mg
Sodium: 41 mg   Calcium: 9 mg
Nutritional Analysis is only for sauce.

Basil Butter Baste

1½ cups whipped unsalted
    butter, slightly softened
3 tablespoons fresh
    chopped basil
1 teaspoon minced garlic
3 tablespoons lemon juice
pinch of salt
pinch of pepper

Serving: 2 Teaspoons   Calories: 55
Protein: 0 gm   Fat: 6 gm
Carbs: 0 gm   Cholesterol: 17 mg
Sodium: 66 mg   Calcium: 2 mg

MAKES 1½ CUPS

Combine all ingredients in the chilled container of a blender or food processor. Very briefly pulse until all are combined, do not allow to run or air will be beaten out of whipped butter. Transfer to covered storage container and chill.

To use, soften to room temperature and brush on grilled meats and vegetables immediately after removing from grill. The light and fluffy characteristic of whipped butter allows you to use less and enjoy more!

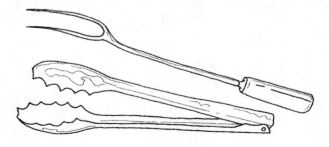

Fuel and Fire

The fuel used to create the fire is an important ingredient in the whole barbecuing process. The best fuel is hardwood charcoal, which is made by burning hardwood until it is dry and porous. It comes from oak, maple, cherry, apple, hickory, mesquite and alder woods, each adding a distinct flavor to the grilling. While the most common fuel is charcoal briquets, these are the least satisfactory. Briquets are scraps of charred wood or sawdust held together with a petroleum product. Some briquets release the terrible smell of oil which can flavor the food, while the best briquets simply smell of burnt wood. When cooking, add aromatic chips to the fire to enhance the smoke and flavor of the grilling.

Lighting the fire requires attention to safety. Obviously, the grill should be kept a good distance from trees, furniture and other combustible articles including garage doors and overhangs. The best method is to use lighter fluid to start the fire since any chemical traces are incinerated in minutes. The use of an electric coil is also a good option. Mound the charcoal into a pyramid in the center and allow it to burn for 30 minutes. When it is evenly covered with a white ash, the fire is ready for grilling. For long-cooking foods, push the embers into a circle on the outer perimeter of the grill to

Maple-Mustard Salmon

1½ lbs. fresh salmon fillets
1 tablespoon ground
   mustard seed
¼ cup maple syrup
1 teaspoon lemon juice
¼ teaspoon salt
1 teaspoon white pepper
1 teaspoon butter, melted

Serving: 1/4 Recipe
Protein: 34 gm
Carbs: 15 gm
Sodium: 233 mg

Calories: 302
Fat: 12 gm
Cholesterol: 96 mg
Calcium: 47 mg

SERVES 4

Prepare grill or preheat broiler. Check fillets for bones, and remove with pliers. Blend mustard, maple syrup, lemon juice, salt and pepper to make sauce.

Remove grill from flames, or broiler pan from heat, and spray with nonstick oil. Place fillets on cooking surface and brush with butter. Coat with maple-mustard sauce. Cover grill or leave oven door tipped open. Salmon is done when inner flesh is light pink. Serve with juices from pan spooned over fish.

Perfect Swordfish

4 swordfish steaks, sized
   to suit appetites
2 tablespoons olive oil
2 tablespoons lemon juice
½ teaspoon tamari or
   soy sauce
1 teaspoon pepper

Serving: 1/4 Recipe
Protein: 34 gm
Carbs: 1 gm
Sodium: 195 mg

Calories: 270
Fat: 13.5 gm
Cholesterol: 66 mg
Calcium: 10 mg

SERVES 4

Cut off any visible fat from swordfish steaks. In a shallow pan, make a marinade of olive oil, lemon juice, tamari or soy sauce and pepper. Soak swordfish steaks in marinade, spooning liquid over tops of steaks. Cover pan, refrigerate at least 1 hour.

Prepare grill or preheat broiler. Remove cooking surface from flames or heat and spray with nonstick oil, for easier cleanup. Place swordfish on grill, or upper oven rack under broiler leaving oven door tipped open. When browned, turn fish steaks, baste with marinade and brown second side. Total cooking time should be 10-12 minutes.

Braised Scallops

1 lb. scallops
1 pint cherry tomatoes
½ cup safflower oil
4 tablespoons vinegar
¼ teaspoon tamari or
    soy sauce
1 teaspoon basil
1 teaspoon pepper
1 teaspoon garlic powder

Serving: 1/4 Recipe
Protein: 20 gm
Carbs: 9 gm
Sodium: 212 mg

Calories: 216
Fat: 11.5 gm
Cholesterol: 37 mg
Calcium: 43 mg

SERVES 4

Wash scallops and cherry tomatoes. In a wide, shallow bowl, mix remaining ingredients to make marinade. Add scallops and tomatoes. Refrigerate at least 2 hours, stirring occasionally. Alternate scallops and tomatoes on skewers. Reserve marinade for basting.

Remove grill from flames and spray with nonstick oil. Place skewers on grill. Depending on heat of coals and size of scallops, cook 8-12 minutes, turning and basting every 2-3 minutes until cooked through.

Marinated Shrimp

1 ½ lbs. medium-sized
   shrimp, peeled and
   deveined

SERVES 4

Preheat grill. Rinse shrimp and pat dry. Blend your choice of baste. Consistency should be thick, but spreadable.

Baste #1
2 tablespoons miso paste
2 tablespoons lemon juice
5 tablespoons red wine

Serving: 1/4 Recipe   Calories: 207
Protein: 35 gm   Fat: 3 gm
Carbs: 5 gm   Cholesterol: 258 mg
Sodium: 374 mg   Calcium: 92 mg
Nutritional Analysis includes shrimp

Remove grill from flames and spray with nonstick oil. Place shrimp on flat, double-edged skewers, with space between them. Coat with baste. Grill, turning shrimp to brown on all sides, and basting as needed. Shrimp will cook in 10-12 minutes.

Baste #2
1 teaspoon tamari or soy sauce
4 tablespoons lemon juice
3 tablespoons flour
4 tablespoons white wine

Serving: 1/4 Recipe   Calories: 216
Protein: 35 gm   Fat: 3 gm
Carbs: 8 gm   Cholesterol: 258 mg
Sodium: 338 mg   Calcium: 92 mg
Nutritional Analysis includes shrimp

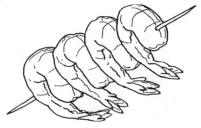

Incredible Trout

SERVES 4

4 trout fillets,
    sized to suit appetites
3 lemons, sliced thin
1 onion, sliced into slivers
4 pinches salt
4 pinches pepper
4 tablespoons chopped
    cilantro sprigs (coriander)
½ cup sliced almonds

Serving: 1/4 Recipe
Protein: 37 gm
Carbs: 11 gm
Sodium: 171 mg

Calories: 308
Fat: 14.5 gm
Cholesterol: 94 mg
Calcium: 193 mg

Make a packet for each serving of trout:
fold a double thickness of aluminum
foil into a 12 inch square. Place trout
in middle of foil and sprinkle with salt
and pepper. Cover with lemon slices
and onion slivers. Sprinkle each serving
with a pinch each of salt and pepper, a
tablespoon cilantro and 2 tablespoons
sliced almonds.

Fold in ends of foil and crease. Bring
sides of foil together over fish, fold edges
together, and crease into a ½ inch seam.
Continue turning and creasing until
seam is flat against fish. Place packet on
grill, cooking 4 minutes on each side.

Stuffed Halibut

SERVES 4

1 teaspoon canola oil
½ cup finely chopped onion
½ teaspoon finely chopped
   fresh hot pepper
1 cup peeled and finely
   chopped apple
3 pinches dried rosemary
2 pinches dried thyme
¼ cup chopped walnuts
1 cup seasoned bread crumbs
1½ lbs. thinly sliced
   halibut fillets
1 tablespoon olive oil

Serving: 1/4 Recipe	Calories: 395
Protein: 42 gm	Fat: 11.5 gm
Carbs: 30 gm	Cholesterol: 55 mg
Sodium: 888 mg	Calcium: 121 mg

Warm oil in a medium frying pan, add onion and pepper, and sauté 10 minutes or until onion is clear.

Mix in apple, rosemary, and thyme. Cover and reduce heat to low. Cook 10 minutes. Remove from heat and stir in walnuts and bread crumbs, mixing well.

Spray fish basket with non-stick oil. Brush fillets with olive oil. Make a layer of halibut fillets on the bottom of basket. Cover with stuffing, then a second layer of fillets. Place basket on grill, cooking about 9-10 minutes on each side, so that bottom fillet flakes easily with a fork. Serve immediately.

Grilling Guidelines

Some guidelines on cooking time, and how to judge when foods are done, may be useful as you embark on your grilling adventures. Birds of all kinds do well on the grill as parts, butterflied or whole. They do tend to dry out as they cook, so baste continuously during grilling. If the skin is left on, poultry should initially be grilled skin side down to the fire and cooked over direct heat in a covered grill. It is done when a thermometer reads 170º - 175º, the meat is opaque and easily separates from the bone, and the juices from the joints run yellow with a trace of pink.

Seafood is sensational on the grill. The hinged fish basket makes turning fish much easier and is highly recommended. Grill steaks, fillets, shrimp and scallops over direct heat. Grill whole fish over indirect heat. Once again, baste regularly to keep fish from drying out, and watch closely because it cooks fast on the grill, no more than 10 minutes per inch of thickness. When cooked, the flesh will be opaque and springy to the touch.

Just about any vegetable can be grilled. Potatoes and corn can be wrapped in aluminum foil and placed in the coals. Eggplant, red onion, summer squash and carrots may be sliced and placed directly over the fire. Keep basting to prevent drying out.

Chicken with Curried Peach Sauce

SERVES 8

6 ripe peaches
2 red onions, finely diced
2 roasted red peppers, finely diced
1 teaspoon minced garlic
3 tablespoons extra virgin olive oil
3 tablespoons balsamic vinegar
4 tablespoons white wine
1 teaspoon curry powder
1½ tablespoons fresh thyme
pinch of salt
pinch of pepper
2 tablespoons lemon juice
8 chicken breasts, skinned

Pit, peel and dice peaches into pieces the size of sugar cubes. In a large saucepan, combine peaches, onions, red peppers, garlic and olive oil. Simmer 10 minutes, then reduce heat and add vinegar, wine, curry, thyme, salt and pepper. Cover pan, and allow mixture to sit at room temperature for 1 hour, then stir in lemon juice.

Remove grill from flames and spray with nonstick oil. Season the chicken with salt and pepper. Grill chicken over medium heat, about 8-10 minutes on each side. Serve grilled chicken smothered in warm Curried Peach Sauce.

Serving: 1/8 Recipe
Protein: 56 gm
Carbs: 15 gm
Sodium: 172 mg

Calories: 372
Fat: 8.5 gm
Cholesterol: 137 mg
Calcium: 65 mg

Rosemary Herbed Chicken

2 tablespoons garlic powder
3 tablespoons minced fresh
   rosemary
5 tablespoons olive oil
pinch of salt
pinch of pepper
2 lbs. lean skinned chicken

Serving: 1/4 Recipe
Protein: 53 gm
Carbs: 4 gm
Sodium: 178 mg

Calories: 330
Fat: 10 gm
Cholesterol: 132 mg
Calcium: 55 mg

SERVES 4

In a small bowl, combine garlic, rosemary, olive oil, salt and pepper. Rub herbed mixture all over chicken.

Remove grill from flames and spray with nonstick oil. Place chicken on the grill, cooking about 8-10 minutes on each side.

To see if chicken is properly cooked, cut into a joint and check to see that the color is completely opaque, with no trace of redness. When removing from grill, brush with any remaining herbed oil.

Jamaican Chicken Jerk

Paste:

½ cup Caribbean hot
    sauce, or pepper sauce
4 tablespoons rosemary
4 tablespoons parsley flakes
4 tablespoons basil
4 tablespoons thyme
4 tablespoons ground
    mustard seeds
6 scallions, finely chopped
¼ teaspoon salt
1 teaspoon black pepper
juice of 2 limes
¼ cup prepared mustard
1 cup orange juice
½ cup red wine vinegar

6 chicken thighs and legs

SERVES 4

Combine all paste ingredients in a food processor, and blend into a paste, checking to be sure they are completely mixed. Transfer to covered container and refrigerate at least 2 hours.

Remove grill from flames and spray with nonstick oil. Rub the paste on the chicken, then place chicken on the grill over very low heat. Turn and baste as needed. If grill is left uncovered, cook chicken about 1 hour. If grill is covered, cook about 30 minutes. Keep heat low during grilling, but do not remove from grill until meat easily pulls away from the bone. Serve with extra jerk sauce.

Serving: 1/4 Recipe
Protein: 4 gm
Carbs: 20 gm
Sodium: 353 mg

Calories: 181
Fat: 4 gm
Cholesterol: 0 mg
Calcium: 254 mg

Crispy Lowfat Chicken

3 egg whites
1 cup unbleached flour
pinch of salt
pinch of pepper
4 chicken breasts, skinned

SERVES 4

Serving: 1/4 Recipe	Calories: 386
Protein: 60 gm	Fat: 3 gm
Carbs: 24 gm	Cholesterol: 137 mg
Sodium: 224 mg	Calcium: 33 mg

In a large bowl, whisk egg whites until frothy. In a small brown bag, combine flour with salt and pepper. Pat chicken dry with a cloth towel, then place in egg whites, turning to coat all sides. Dredge in bag of flour, then set on wax paper.

Remove grill from flames and spray with nonstick oil. Allow flames to burn down to hot coals. Place chicken on hot grill, turning to brown on each side. Make an incision before removing from the grill to check that meat is opaque on the inside with no trace of redness.

Oriental Grill

Oriental Sauce:

½ cup rice wine vinegar
¼ cup roasted unsalted
   peanuts, crushed
¼ teaspoon salt
2 tablespoons fresh basil
2 tablespoons fresh cilantro
2 tablespoons lemongrass
1 teaspoon chili sauce
4 tablespoons lime juice

2 lbs. skinned chicken,
   cut into 3-inch strips
1 lb. carrots, peeled and
   cut into thick strips
1 eggplant, peeled and cut
   into thick strips
½ lb. whole black mushrooms
8 scallions, white part only

SERVES 4

Combine sauce ingredients and process in blender or food processor for 2 minutes. Toss prepared chicken and vegetables in sauce.

Remove grill from flames and spray with nonstick oil. Place meat and carrots on grill. When ready to turn, put remaining vegetables on grill, placing to keep them from falling through as they are reduced in size.

Remove grilled items as they are cooked through, and keep warm in an oven. Before serving, pour remaining Oriental Sauce over all.

Serving: 1/4 Recipe
Protein: 58 gm
Carbs: 24 gm
Sodium: 431 mg

Calories: 413
Fat: 8 gm
Cholesterol: 132 mg
Calcium: 83 mg

Hobo Campfire Packs

1 lb. lean skinned chicken
1 large sweet potato,
    quartered
6 cloves garlic, peeled and
    horizontally halved
1 large onion, peeled and
    quartered
1 large tomato, quartered
2 ears of corn, husked and
    cut into halves
1 large carrot, peeled and
    cut into large chunks
2 rosemary sprigs
pinch of salt
pinch of pepper
1 teaspoon butter

Serving: 1/2 Recipe
Protein: 58 gm
Carbs: 50 gm
Sodium: 267 mg

Calories: 483
Fat: 6.5 gm
Cholesterol: 137 mg
Calcium: 94 mg

Arrange half of the chicken meat in a single layer on a large sheet of extra-heavy-duty aluminum foil. Arrange half of the vegetables and a sprig of rosemary around chicken. Salt, pepper and dot a half a teaspoon of butter over all. Place another large sheet of foil on top. Fold, crease and roll the edges of the sheets together, and continue folding until folds are up against ingredients. However, be careful not to mound up the food inside or it will not cook through. Cover the entire pack with another layer of foil. Repeat process with remaining chicken and vegetables.

Build a campfire, let it burn down to hot coals, and place the packs on the hot embers. Arrange coals around packs. Use 2 spatulas to carefully turn after 25 minutes, cook 20 minutes more. Adjust cooking time to heat of the fire.

New England Lobster Bake

1 can of beer
6 cups sea water
6 dozen steamer clams
6 lobsters, 1¼-1½ lbs.
6 ears of corn, husked

Hot Lemon Butter Sauce:
1 tablespoon butter, melted
¾ cup liquid from steamed
   lobsters and clams
3 tablespoons lemon juice

Serving: 1/6 Recipe
Protein: 60 gm
Carbs: 27 gm
Sodium: 675 mg

Calories: 409
Fat: 6.5 gm
Cholesterol: 224 mg
Calcium: 180 mg

SERVES 6

Pour beer and water in a 24-quart steamer. Cover and bring to a full boil.

Scrub clams, discarding any with broken shells or that do not close tightly when handled. Place clams, by the dozen, in squares of cheesecloth and tie with string. Allow room in bags for clams to open.

Place lobsters and corn in steaming pot. Cover. After 15 minutes, add steamer bags. Cover and steam until clams open, about 15 minutes.

In a saucepan, combine ingredients for Hot Lemon Butter Sauce, simmer 10 minutes. Serve sauce in dipping bowls.

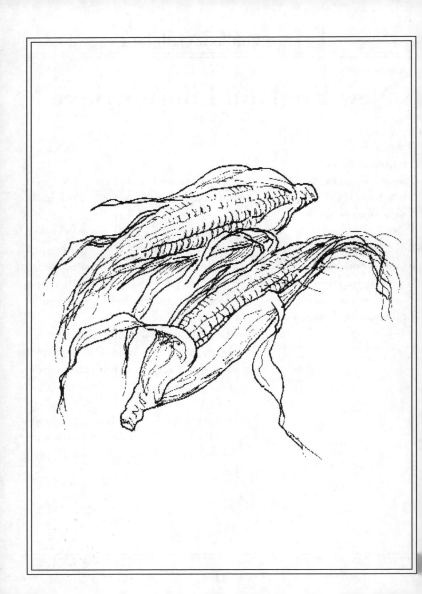